CW00495626

Words for Feasts & Saints Days

by
Bishop Hugh Gilbert, OSB

*All booklets are published thanks to the
generous support of the members of the
Catholic Truth Society*

CATHOLIC TRUTH SOCIETY
PUBLISHERS TO THE HOLY SEE

Contents

All rights reserved. First published 2015 by The Incorporated Catholic Truth Society, 40-46 Harleyford Road London SE11 5AY Tel: 020 7640 0042 Fax: 020 7640 0046. © 2015 The Incorporated Catholic Truth Society.

ISBN 978 1 78469 061 8

Introduction

The liturgical year - with its Sundays and weekdays, Easter and Christmas, Advent and Lent, Ordinary time, ferias and feasts - is one of the great givens of the Christian life. We live our lives within it. This is true even when we are not consciously referring to it. It's a framework, a mould, a supporting rhythm, a background that at some peak times becomes the foreground. It has, too, been one of the great facts of European and Western cultural history. We're familiar with the civil year (which comes to us from the Romans), the financial year, the academic year ... But there is this other presence too, still hanging on even in semi-pagan Britain - and every revolutionary attempt to conjure it away (1789, 1917) has itself foundered.

In the Roman Rite now, we have a liturgical year both luminously intent on the essentials and rich in its details. "By means of the yearly cycle," says the Calendarium Romanum of 1969, echoing Vatican II's *Sacrosanctum Concilium,* "the Church celebrates the whole mystery of Christ, from his Incarnation until the day of Pentecost and the expectation of his coming again."

The Presentation of the Lord

Behold, he comes to his holy temple, our Lord and Master: come, let us adore him (Invitatory Antiphon for the feast of the Presentation of the Lord).

Forty days after his birth, in the arms of his mother, the Lord comes to his temple, fulfilling the prophecy of Malachi, and other prophecies besides. He comes to his temple to build the true Temple, the temple not made with hands, unless it be the hands outstretched on the Cross. The feast of the Presentation, like that of the Epiphany in a different way, is about the Church. The Lord reveals himself, and the issue is the Church. The Lord comes and opens up this new, broad place, no longer of restricted access, like the Jerusalem Temple, but open to all who have faith in Christ. Suddenly, there is *Lebensraum*, Catholicism.

And in this new Temple, this new space, the new worship comes into being. This too is the fulfilment of the prophecy of Malachi: "For he is like a refiner's fire and like fuller's soap; he will sit as refiner and purifier of silver, and he will purify the sons of Levi and refine them like gold and silver, till they present right offerings to the Lord. Then the offering of Judah and Jerusalem will be pleasing to the Lord as in the days of old and as in former years" (*Ml* 3:2-4). This new, pleasing worship is adumbrated in Mary and Joseph. They bring the offering of the poor, "a pair of turtle-doves or two young pigeons" (*Lk* 2:24). Essentially they bring their poverty of spirit: their openness to the word of God that the Holy Spirit will speak through Simeon and Anna. They bring their willingness to learn more about the child they are carrying, and to enter into his paschal mystery. For "this child is set for the fall and rising of many in Israel, and for a sign that is spoken against (and a sword will pierce your own soul also)" (*Lk* 2:34-35). This is the new worship while Paul will solemnly intone, as it were, at the beginning of Romans 12: "I appeal to you, therefore, brethren, by the mercies of God, to present your bodies as a living sacrifice, holy and acceptable to God, which is your reasonable (*logikos*) worship" (*Rm* 12:1). Joseph Ratzinger/Pope Benedict makes this text the Invitatory Antiphon, so to speak, of Christian worship as such. It is striking that Mary and Joseph come to Jerusalem to "present" their child to the Lord, and St Paul bids the Romans to "present" their bodies. And Mary and

Joseph come - the second thing Luke mentions - "to offer a sacrifice", and St Paul says, "present your bodies as a living sacrifice". The gestures of Mary and Joseph, still within the parameters of the old Law, anticipate remarkably the worship of the new.

Going forth to meet him

The Lord comes to his temple, Herod's temple, that deeply ambivalent place, and there, tiny and silent, he begins to build the new Temple and initiate the new worship, which is his, his paschal Mystery.

In this feast, and its Invitatory, there's a movement, a double movement. On the one hand, the Lord comes. On the other hand, Sion, Simeon and Anna, the Church runs to meet him. There's the approach of the Lord, his Advent, and there is our going forth to meet him. The second movement answering the first.

Our whole life is lived within this. And the liturgy especially. God comes close to us every day, and we approach him. "What was visible in our Redeemer has passed over into the mysteries", said St Leo. The Lord, risen and ascended, still comes to us. He comes to us in the "mysteries", the sacramental life of the Church. And so we can say with St Ambrose, "I find you in your mysteries." Thus, as the Benedictine abbot Bl. Columba Marmion would say, "the mysteries of Christ [become] our mysteries." They enter into us and we into them.

These sacramental mysteries include Holy Scripture, the Sacraments in the strict sense, the Divine Office, icons and images, churches and their furnishings, and, not least, the 'sacramental' we call the liturgical year. In all of these, in differing ways, the one transforming mystery of Christ's death and resurrection comes to us and we can run forth to meet it. What a joy it is when children run to meet you, when they throw themselves at you. Isn't this a joy we could give the Lord? He is our Father and we are his children. He comes in his mysteries, and we can't hold back. We rush to him. But what draws us is the presence in the Mysteries.

And, not least, in the round of feasts. Dom Gregory Collins puts it well: "As we celebrate our feasts, the Holy Spirit renders Jesus present in our worship as the sacrificed and glorified Saviour, the High Priest of the new and everlasting covenant. Through the liturgy, the grace and power of the original event is reactivated and shared afresh with us ... In the liturgy, Christ carries out his priestly work among us, making present once again the power of the love by which he saved us, and opening up once more the great mystery for our participation through the joy and beauty of the feast" (*Meeting Christ in his Mysteries*). And so Christ is born for us and in us at Christmas. At Epiphany he is made manifest and we are illumined. At his Baptism and the changing of the water into wine, he lets his glory be seen, and we like his first disciples can believe in him. At the Presentation he comes to his Temple and we become his Temple. "On Good Friday we die spiritually with him and on Holy Saturday we are buried with him, interring him spiritually in our hearts. On Easter Sunday we celebrate his rising and we rise with him as well, experiencing the explosion of an indestructible new life and an inexpressible joy within ourselves. In celebrating his ascension into glory, we experience our being carried up by him on high and enthroned with him in the heavenly places" (ibid).

Interiorising the mystery

"Christ Himself", wrote Newman, "vouchsafes to repeat in each of us in figure and mystery all that He did and suffered in the flesh. He is formed in us, born in us, suffers in us, rises again in us, lives in us ... He comes to us as a Spirit, all dying, all rising, all living" (*Parochial and Plain Sermons* V, pp. 138-9).

Through the Eucharist, each day of our life becomes a 'place', a 'time', a Temple, in which Christ celebrates his advent, his death and resurrection, his sending of the Spirit, and even, in anticipation, his return in glory. Through the grace of Sunday, each week becomes this. Thanks to the liturgical year, Easter above all, each year of our life becomes it. Through the Sacrament of Baptism, by which we die and rise in Christ, our whole life, each event that comprises it, its different phases, its own rising and declining, becomes this holy place in which, through the Holy Spirit, God and man meet, and Christ celebrates his mysteries. And 'celebrate', in the early Church, meant 'accomplish'. Personal prayer, in turn, can be described as "interiorising the mystery".

"All things are twofold, one opposite the other, and he has made nothing incomplete. O ne confirms the good things of the other, and who can have enough of beholding his glory?" (*Si* 42:24-25). God's glory is beheld in the Temple, this Temple, the building of which is the innermost meaning of history, the Church. And God's glory becomes visible there in the twofoldness of things, one opposite the other, each confirming the good things of the other. This is precisely what we see in the Gospel account. An old man holds a young child in his arms. Joseph and Mary are young, Simeon and Anna are old. There are two men, two women. Christ is declared "the light of revelation to the Gentiles and glory to your people Israel". The Church, the monastery, the praying, Catholic heart is not only a place where God meets man and man God, but, because of that, a place where young and old, male and female, Jew and Gentile meet each other, and confirm the good things of each other. And so God's glory is seen. The devil loves to infiltrate, his smoke entering the Temple, as Paul VI said. He loves to set brother against brother. He loves to point out to us each other's little faults, he loves to create false impressions, sow distrust, misgivings, fear. He prowls around. We have to guard our hearts, to keep them ecclesial, Catholic. Whenever we close ourselves to a brother or sister, we close down part of ourselves, and therefore part of our hearts to God. His glory can no longer dwell there. The 'Advent' is less than it could have been. "Pray, then, come and join this choir, every one of you; let there be a whole symphony of minds in concert; take the tone altogether from God, and sing aloud to the Father with one voice through Jesus Christ, so that He may hear you and know by your good works that you are indeed members of His Son's Body. A completely united front will help to keep you in constant communion with God" (Ignatius of Antioch, *Ephesians* 4).

May this feast, then, do its work in us. May we be grateful for this new space the Lord has opened for us and live in it always. And allow each other space as well.

The Holy Trinity

With last Sunday, Pentecost, the Easter season came to an end. Through Advent, Christmas, Lent and Easter the Church has been reliving redemption, stage by stage: the coming of the Son, the mysteries of his life, death and resurrection, and - their fruit - the coming of the Holy Spirit. But now those days have gone: the Church's four seasons have run their course. What, we wonder, happens next? What does the Church do now?

She keeps, in swift succession, three great feasts: today's feast of the Holy Trinity, next Thursday's feast of Corpus Christi and, at the end of the following week, the feast of the Sacred Heart.[1]

These three feasts go together. They are all of more recent foundation than the great feasts of Christmas and Easter. Whereas those last go back to the early centuries of the Church, we owe the feasts of the Trinity and Corpus Christi to the Middle Ages and that of the Sacred Heart to the seventeenth century. But they go together, above all, because they have a common purpose. They each in a different way do the same thing. It is as if the Church, after the drama of her four seasons, pauses for a moment and draws breath. She looks back along the road she has travelled since Advent, the road of redemption, and she seeks to sum up what that journey was about. She is so full of the gift she has received that, as it were, she turns it over and over in her hands, looking at it from different sides and trying to describe to herself what it is. She goes to the essentials of her redemption, its first principles, its source, its heart, and rests there, grateful.

Therefore, naturally, the Church turns to the consecrated bread and wine, the Eucharist, because in the Eucharist Christ is continually renewing our redemption in its fullness; and so we have the feast of the Body and Blood of Christ. She turns to the pierced Heart of her Saviour, running with the blood and water of redemption; and so we have the feast of Christ's Sacred Heart. But, first of all, as is right, she turns to the Holy Trinity. She turns to the source and centre and end of her redemption, the God who was and who is and who is to come, the Almighty; and so we have this feast, the feast of the triune God.

Knowing, loving and serving them

St Ignatius Loyola, who founded the Jesuits, was at the end of his life so full of the thought of the Trinity that he could not see three people, three apples, three books or three anything, without falling into an ecstasy. St Maximilian Kolbe, when in Auschwitz, would gather his fellow-prisoners round him on a Sunday and talk to them. These were starving, exhausted, degraded men, men condemned to a horrible death, many of them not Catholics, not even Christians, and they would listen spellbound to his every word. What did he talk about? He talked about the relationship of Our Lady to the Three Persons of the Holy Trinity.

Like the saints, then, the Church turns, above all, to the Trinity. She turns to the Trinity because the Trinity is her redemption. Redemption, we know, has two sides, God's and ours. It is, on one side, something God does for us: *God* redeems; and, on the other, it is something that happens to us: *we* are redeemed. It begins as the mercy of God and ends as a change in us.

And from whichever side we look at it, we see that it is all about the Trinity.

On God's side, it is "the grace of our Lord, Jesus Christ, the love of God and the fellowship of the Holy Spirit". On our side, it is a relationship to those three Persons, a knowing, loving and serving of them. On God's side, it is God so loving the world as to give his only Son, God sending the Spirit of his Son into our hearts. On our side, it is having that Son in our hearts by faith and, in the Spirit, crying "Abba, Father". On God's side, it is God coming to us in hidden glory, God giving himself fully, as Father, Son and Holy Spirit: as the Father, source of all life; as the co-eternal Son, the perfect copy of the Father, true God from true God and one with him; as the Holy Spirit, the bond between Father and Son, the Spirit of them both, their love and Peace in person, one God with them. On our side, it is being, by baptism, a son of the Father, a member of Christ, a temple of the Holy Spirit.

Feast of Redemption

This is why there is a feast of the Holy Trinity and why it falls when it does. The Church is basking, as it were, in the finished work of her redemption. Easter is over, the Son ascended, the Spirit sent; and the Church falls prostrate in adoration before the all-holy God, her Maker, Redeemer and Sanctifier: Father, Son and Holy Spirit, our redemption.

A last thought is this: when the Church turns to the Holy Trinity, she turns to rest.

The Church has sounded the depths of her redemption and is at peace. That peace is the Trinity. Summer brings work, but the Church takes this summer Sunday and spends it saying one thing only: Glory be to the Father and to the Son and to the Holy Spirit. She rests in adoration. She allows herself a foretaste of the eternal rest to come. She contemplates the rest of God himself.

"Turn, my soul, to your rest, for the Lord has done good to you", says a psalm. "Let us strive to enter this rest", "the Sabbath rest which remains to the people of God", the rest of the Father in the Son and the Son in the Father and the Holy Spirit in them both. Amen.

Corpus Christi

Say to the owner of the house: "The Master says: Where is my room, where I can eat the Passover with my disciples?" He will show you a large upper room furnished with couches, all prepared.

"Where is my room, where I can eat the Passover with my disciples?"

Lord Jesus Christ, here is your room. Here you can eat the Passover with your disciples. Here you can fulfil the desire of your heart. Yes, this is where we are: in this upper room. This is where we are every time we take part in the Mass. And it's where we are particularly today and the focus of our hearts is on the great mystery at the heart of our Christian faith and life: the holy Eucharist.[2]

We are in the Upper Room, we are close to the heart of Christ. And time and space are spirited away. And Christ is all and in all. Christ and the Church, one body, one great mystery. The one enduring reality, Christ wanting to eat the Passover with his disciples.

Let us then, in this Upper Room, on this feast of Corpus Christi, look at Jesus. Look at what he did that night, look at what he does - through the ministry of priests - every time Mass is celebrated. The Benedictine abbot Bl. Columba Marmion had once been saying an unscheduled Mass. He had just unvested in the sacristy, when in burst an irate sacristan. "Who's been saying Mass?" he demanded. Abbot Marmion replied: "Jesus Christ."

"As they were eating, he took some bread ... he took a cup." This is the first thing Jesus did: he took some of the bread of the Passover Meal, he took one of the cups of wine. Fruit of the earth, fruit of the vine, and the work of human hands. He took them into his hands: gifts of God and staples of life, the bread that strengthens man's heart and the wine that gives it joy - simple and precious things. It's what is done at every Mass at the preparation of the gifts of offertory, and we know it's a moment for putting ourselves and our lives into the hands of Christ.

Thanksgiving in the Eucharist

"He took some bread, and ... said the blessing ... he took a cup, and ... returned thanks." This is the second thing that Jesus did: he blessed God, he thanked God. He was celebrating the Jewish Passover, remembering God's great act of liberation at the Exodus and the covenant that followed it. He blessed and thanked God for the history of Israel and for creation. But more than that: he blessed and thanked God for what God the Father was about to do through him. We are, let's remember, in the Upper Room. We are in the night before he suffered. Jesus is about to begin his Passover from this world to the Father. A new covenant between God and man is about to be forged through the death and resurrection of Christ: a new order of relationships, a new beginning, a new creation, the fulfilment of prophecy and history. Looking beyond his own sufferings, Christ thanks and blesses God for all of this. This is why we talk of Eucharist; thanksgiving. In the Mass, every Mass, we, the Church, are taken up into this thanking and blessing of Christ. "Lift up your hearts. We lift them up to the Lord. Let us give thanks to the Lord our God. It is right and just. Father in heaven, we do well always and everywhere to give you thanks." "Through Christ, with Christ, in Christ", we thank and bless and praise and glorify God the Father for all his blessings, for all that he has done and is doing and will do: creating, redeeming, glorifying. Saying "sorry" and saying "thank you" are two human basics. We learn them, please God, as children. They're the two great remedies of our pride. And in the sacraments we lift these phrases to the Father. We say sorry in confession and so are reconciled. We say thank you in the Mass - following the grateful Christ.

His sacrifice embodied

We are in the Upper Room. We are watching Christ. He has taken the bread, taken the cup. He has blessed and thanked. And now, thirdly, he speaks those momentous words: Take this, this is my body which is given up for you ... This is my blood, the blood of the covenant, which is to be poured out for many. Something unheard of is happening here, something a child can understand and believe and yet something that the greatest minds will never stop exploring. Christ changes the bread into his body. He changes the wine into his blood. And it is the body given for us, the blood shed for us. This meal to which Christ invites us, this Christian Passover he longs to eat with us, is a sacrificial meal. Our Lord, on the eve of his Passion, on the night on which he was betrayed, anticipated in this ritual way the sacrifice of himself he would make on the Cross the following day. He embodied himself and his sacrifice in the bread and wine of the Last Supper.

He translated his sacrifice, as it were, into this simple language and gave it to the Church to celebrate in his memory. And so it is that in the Eucharist, the sacrifice Christ offered once for all on the Cross remains present throughout time, and we can draw near to it. We can draw life and strength from it. We can be caught up in the gift of himself Jesus made to the Father. "May he make us, we pray, an everlasting gift to You." May Christ make us, the Church, an everlasting gift to the Father. We can intercede with Christ for each other, for the whole world, for those who have died in the peace of Christ. We find ourselves one with Mary and the saints in heaven. They are fully the gift we are becoming through the power of Christ's sacrifice present in the Mass.

We are in the Upper Room. We are watching Christ. He has taken, he has blessed, he has spoken the words and made himself and his sacrifice present. And now, fourthly, lastly, he breaks the bread and gives it to his disciples, he gives them the cup to drink. It's the moment we call Holy Communion. "Truly, I say to you, unless you eat the flesh of the Son of man and drink his blood, you have no life in you." We receive the body and blood of Christ. We receive Christ himself. We receive the body and blood of the Son of God made man. The mystery of the Incarnation is taken through to its ultimate point and Christ eats the Passover with his disciples. (And we can become what we receive.) It's a great and holy moment and we must prepare ourselves for it. If we are conscious of grave sin, we must first receive the absolution of the Sacrament of Reconciliation. If we are not, we must still, as St Paul, discern the body: come with faith and humility and reverence. "Lord, I am not worthy that you should enter under my roof, but only say the word and my soul shall be healed." When the priest holds the host before us, and says "The Body of Christ", we should say "Amen. So it is", with our whole hearts. And then we will become what we receive.

Christ is with us

We will find ourselves, each of us, members of Christ, and all together, the body of Christ. Our whole lives will be changed from within. We will have a new strength and a new joy. We will be able to love where we thought love was impossible. Our eyes will be opened and we will see Christ everywhere. We will see him in our spouses and children and colleagues. We will see him in the Horn of Africa, poor and hungry, and feed him. We will see him in the Church and we will be happy when occasion is given, as it is today, to adore him present in the Eucharist that we receive. We will long for his coming in glory, when the Mass will turn into heaven.

Today we are in the Upper Room. And it is good for us to be here. Christ is with us. After his Resurrection, he returned to this room, and said "Peace be with you", the words with which a bishop opens the Mass. And later, we will leave this Upper Room. But, please God, something will have happened. It was in the Upper Room too that, after Jesus's Ascension, the first Christians were gathered together, and it was there that the Holy Spirit fell on them in wind and fire. That, too, is part of the mystery of the Upper Room and of holy Mass. Jesus offers himself and us to the Father and the Father responds with the Spirit. Jesus gives us his body and hidden in that body is the wind and fire of the Holy Spirit.

Lord Jesus Christ, as you fill us today with your Body and the wonder of its presence, fill us also with your Spirit and send us out in the wind and fire of Pentecost.

The Sacred Heart
of Jesus

Today we are keeping the feast of the Sacred Heart of Jesus.[3] We have been living through the two great liturgical cycles of Christmas and Easter, following Jesus from his conception and birth to his Ascension and the sending of the Holy Spirit. We have been taking part in the unfolding story of our redemption, ever old and ever new. Today, as it were, the liturgy shows us - Christ shows us - the heart of that whole Gospel story. We are shown, we see, what really drives it, fuels it, what made it happen: the love of God made visible in Christ. The human heart of our Saviour, Jesus.

Here's a fine passage from Vatican II: "By his incarnation, he, the Son of God, has in a certain way united himself with each human being. He worked with human hands, he thought with a human mind, he acted with a human will, *and he loved with a human heart*" (*Gaudium et Spes* 22). Notice how that is left to the last: "he loved with a human heart". "You have kept the best wine until now."

Here's the Catechism: "Jesus knew and loved us each and all during his life, his agony and his Passion, and gave himself up for each one of us: 'The Son of God ... loved me and gave himself for me.' He has loved us all with a human heart. For this reason, the Sacred Heart of Jesus, pierced by our sin and for our salvation, 'is quite rightly considered the chief sign and symbol of that ... love with which the divine Redeemer continually loves the eternal Father and all human beings' without exception" (*Catechism of the Catholic Church* 478). And again, "It is 'love to the end' that confers on Christ's sacrifice its value as redemption and reparation, as atonement and satisfaction. He knew and loved us all when he offered his life" (*CCC* 616).

Christ's love is certain

What the Church celebrates today is this love of Christ, this love that was there from the beginning and goes to the end. It's there before us. It's at work in our lives now. And it awaits us in the future - "the best is yet to be."

We often wonder, even about our nearest and dearest, "Do they really love me?" "Will they always love me?" One day a wife turns to a husband or vice versa, and says, "I don't love you any more." This happens. What do others have in their hearts regarding us? We don't know. They don't know perhaps. We're all changeable. But Jesus is the rock. Christ's love is certain. We only have to look at the Cross. "What proves that God loves us is that Christ died for us while we were still sinners."

What is it that lies at the heart of things? Is it darkness? We have all had the feeling of being sucked into a black hole, of our life running away from us, or spiralling down into blackness. Do we all just go into the dark? Is that what there is? Are we just bubbles? We expand and then, more or less gracefully, more or less slowly or suddenly, we burst. And we're gone. Is that it? Today's feast allows us to say "No." Beyond "the heart of darkness", at the truest heart of things, is the burning personal love of Christ, the Son of God.

In today's readings - from Year C - the Sacred Heart is shown to be the heart of a shepherd. A story is told of King Baudouin of the Belgians, a holy man. He was visiting a country in North Africa. He saw a shepherd. He stopped the car and went to speak with him. "What do you think of during the day?" he asked. "God and my sheep," said the shepherd.

And so it is with our Lord. His heart is full of his Father and of us.

Heart speaks to heart

I'd like to propose three practical things:

1. Say to Jesus, "I believe you love me."

2. Try to live at the level of the heart. I knew a monk who always tried to make every conversation deep and meaningful. It was too much! There is a place

for football and the weather and all the rest. But, on the other hand, human relations are not meant to be simply superficial. Even if we talk of less important things, we want to communicate at the level of the heart. "Heart speaks to heart."

3. Then there is the Gospel. We're all shepherds. We all have sheep to care for in some sense. Think of one who is a little lost - and reach out. Before you go to bed tonight think of someone, pray for them, and if there's a chance contact them.

It will be Christ's heart going out to them.

The Birthday of John the Baptist

24th June

"**H**is name is John" (*Lk* 1:63). Why do we keep the birthday, the earthly birthday, of John? We heard one answer in the first reading: "The Lord called me before I was born; from my mother's womb he pronounced my name" (*Is* 49:1). And in the first reading of the Vigil Mass: "Before I formed you in the womb I knew you; before you came to birth I consecrated you. I have appointed you as prophet to the nations" (*Jr* 1:5). God knew John, God had conceived the thought of John, God had predestined John, from all eternity. God in his goodness gave him to this elderly infertile couple, and filled him with the Holy Spirit even from his mother's womb. "He will be called John," said Elizabeth (*Lk* 1:60). "His name is John", wrote Zechariah. They were echoing God's thought: it was the name given by the angel nine months before (see *Lk* 1:13). It was the name God the Father had given this child in eternity.

Why keep the earthly birthday of John? Because everything in him: his conception, his leaping in Elizabeth's womb when Mary visited with Jesus in hers, his birth, his time in the desert, his preaching and baptising, his death - everything is full of the Holy Spirit, alive with God, everything is a gift to us, everything is for the Church. His whole life. The mystery and power of this great figure. A monk, centuries ago, said John's voice is "an everlasting voice". And Origen said that the spirit of John is always at work in the world. John, after Mary, is the closest to the risen Christ and therefore closest to us.

God gives laughter and joy

The human race begins when the first man and the first woman become one flesh: so Genesis. The people of Israel begin when Abraham and Sarah have Isaac, despite their age. "God has given me cause to laugh," cries Sarah; "all those who hear of it will laugh with me" (*Gn* 21:6). Isn't it striking that the story of the new humanity, the new Israel, begins with a birth: John's? "And when her neighbours and relations heard that the Lord had shown so great a kindness, they shared her joy" (*Lk* 1:58). Elizabeth laughs. Pope John Paul II famously wrote: "the future of humanity passes by way of the family." God himself passes by way of the family. Abraham and Sarah, an elderly childless couple; Zechariah and Elizabeth the same.

Is there any family that isn't, sometimes anyway, home to tears, to sadness or grief, some pain, some lack, some loss, some brokenness. But God passes by way of the family. God gives life where hope has died. God gives laughter and joy. "His name is John." God is faithful to the word of his original blessing: "be fruitful and multiply" (*Gn* 1:28). God gives life, again and again, conception after conception. God gives life even where there is no life. He gives a child to Abraham and Sarah, to Zechariah and Elizabeth. Even more amazingly, he gives a child to a virgin, without a man being involved at all. "And you will call his name, Jesus" (*Lk* 1:31). All of these things point to the greatest life-giving of all, the raising of the crucified and buried one, the resurrection of our Lord Jesus Christ, the first-born from the dead, the beginning of the new creation. So this little / great miracle with which the Gospel opens, this birth of John, can come as a comfort to every family. John, who gave joy to his mother and father, can encourage all whose vocation it is to marry and raise a family. God passes this way. If he doesn't give physical life or takes it away, he can give another level of life as well, a richness of spirit, a widening of the heart, a capacity to comfort, another kind of parenting.

"His name is John." I think we Europeans need to hear this especially. Without the faith, it has been said, Europe will die. Europe will die if Europeans lack the faith, hope, and love to have children. The future of Europe passes by way of the family. God passes by way of the love of man and woman and the life that comes from it. There are so many reasons for refusing that life, so many means for doing so. But if we turn our back on it, as a society, a civilisation, we die.

"Meanwhile", the Gospel goes on, "the child grew up and his spirit matured. And he lived out in the wilderness until the day he appeared openly to Israel" (*Lk* 1:80). Here's a second striking thing. This son, like Mary's son, like Jesus, didn't marry. He didn't raise a family. God, the life-giving God, passes this way too, through the wilderness, the solitude of singleness. "The friend of the Bridegroom", John called himself (*Jn* 3:29). He was tasked with "preparing a people fit for the Lord" (*Lk* 1:17), preparing the Bride who is the Church for her husband Christ. John didn't marry: he was called to serve what marriage symbolises. "He who is joined to the Lord becomes one spirit with him" (*1 Co* 6:17). And this was his joy. "The bride is only for the bridegroom; and yet the bridegroom's friend, who stands there and listens, is glad when he hears the bridegroom's voice. This same joy I feel, and now it is complete. He must grow greater. I must grow smaller" (*Jn* 3:29-30). When at the banks of the Jordan, John grew smaller and gave way to Jesus and baptised him, he was letting the Bridegroom find the Bride. He was letting him go down into the waters of human suffering to lift us out of them. He was opening the way to the union of God and man in the body of Christ, and the life of the world to come. There, we are told, there will be neither marrying nor giving in marriage, and God will be all in all. So John comes as a comfort too to all those who, by choice, or by necessity, inner or outer, are alone. He encourages all whose vocation involves singleness, celibacy. John's spirit is still at work in the world in this way, too. The loving, life-giving God passes this way also. And the house of love has many mansions.

Courage in Christian witness

And so to the end. It wasn't a happy ending, humanly speaking. We know the story. Herod's birthday, Herod drunk, aroused by the dancing of Salome, promising recklessly, and Herodias seizing her chance. How *she* must have laughed! "The head of John the Baptist on a dish" (*Mt* 14:8). What a delicious dish for her, that everlasting voice everlastingly silenced. It's a horrible story. And here I think John comes for us all. He encourages us in our common Christian witness. We share a situation with him. Why was John in prison? The Herod concerned, a son of the Herod who had had the baby boys in Bethlehem murdered, had been in Rome on one occasion. And there he had met Herodias, the wife of one of his half-brothers. The two fell wildly in love, and eventually married. There were three things wrong with this marriage. First, they were both already married; second, Herodias was Herod's niece; and third, it was against the Law of Moses to marry your brother's wife. This was what John underscored. "It is not lawful to take your brother's wife" (*Mk* 6:18). John said that and took the consequences.

The contemporary relevance is clear. Not every love is entitled to sexual expression. We all know that. Not every love is entitled to the dignity of marriage. We all know that, too. Politically, Herod's 'marriage' to Herodias caused chaos. And so will the changes proposed to the understanding of marriage. Love has many mansions, but marriage is the only true home of sexual love. And marriage is between a man and a woman free to marry, not between anyone else. And here's a third extraordinary thing. This single man, this prophet of the Coming One, didn't die directly for Christ. He died to uphold the truth of marriage. We are called, here and now, in this country, to uphold the very same. We're called not just to think it, but to pray it, say it and write it.

"His name is John". He's a wonderful gift of God, alive in Christ, close to us. In this Eucharist, we can lift up our hearts and give thanks for him. We hear his everlasting voice at every Mass: "Behold the Lamb of God, behold him who takes away the sins of the world." And if we go out from here with his fire in our hearts, the rain won't have mattered at all, and our pilgrimage will have been worthwhile.

St John the Baptist, pray for the married, pray for the single, pray for all of us!

Solemnity of Saints Peter and Paul

29th June

The Church is a city, a building, a house, a temple, our home. And it's built, after Christ, on the foundation of the twelve apostles. They were chosen by Jesus. The New Testament gives their names: Simon Peter (always first); Andrew his brother; James and John, the sons of Zebedee; Philip, Bartholomew, Thomas, Matthew, another James; Thaddaeus, Simon the Zealot and Judas Iscariot (see *Mt* 10:2-4). Judas fell away and Matthias replaced him. Barnabas is also called an apostle. And then, quite freely, the risen and ascended Jesus showed himself to Saul the persecutor, and made him Paul the Apostle. So, Peter the first and Paul the "last" (*1 Co* 15:8). Peter the fisherman, the rock, the key-holder, the shepherd, the first to see the risen Christ, Peter sent to the people of Israel. Paul, the "one untimely born" (*1 Co* 15:8), the chosen vessel, the untiring missionary, the Apostle of the Gentiles. Peter and Paul, the book-ends, as it were, of the College of Apostles, and in between them all the rest. Peter and Paul, both guided by God to Rome, both martyred there, Peter crucified, Paul beheaded, and both since the third century AD at least, venerated together on this day.

Do we, I wonder, appreciate them? Take the apostles out of Christianity, and there'd be nothing left. How poorer it would be, for example, without the personality of Peter, so warm-hearted, impulsive, Peter who has left us the great gift of his own failure and Christ's forgiveness. Peter who said, "You are the Christ, the Son of the living God"; who said, "Lord, to whom can we go? You have the words of everlasting life"; who said, "Lord, you know everything; you know that I love you." What can't we learn from someone like that? Imagine Christianity without Paul: short and bandy-legged (see *Acts Paul* 3), passionate, tender, ironic, sarcastic, loving, always praying, another man who needed forgiveness; Paul of journeys and places - Antioch, Ephesus, Corinth and the rest - with his extraordinary letters, still being read and argued over and shaping Christian thought. Paul, who said, "I live now, not I, but Christ lives in me"; or again, "Who shall separate us from the love of Christ? Shall tribulation or distress or persecution or famine or nakedness or peril or sword? ... No, in all these things we are more than conquerors through him who loved us";

who said, "when I am weak, then I am strong." We see how the Holy Spirit doesn't take personality away, but makes it flower. But there's more than this.

A public witness of the Resurrection

All the divine gifts we enjoy in the Church, *everything* that makes up the New Covenant, comes to us from Christ through the apostles. They were the men appointed by him, to be with him, to imbibe him, as it were. They were the men sent out - that's what 'apostle' means - to proclaim the Gospel and cast out demons, to pass Christ on. They ate and drank with him after his Resurrection and the Holy Spirit came on them in tongues of fire. Take them away and there's nothing left. There'd be no New Testament; it was written by them and their colleagues. There'd be no Eucharist, no Mass; it was the apostles Jesus told, "do this in memory of me". There'd be no forgiveness of sins; it was to them Jesus said, "those whose sins you forgive they are forgiven, those whose sins you retain they are retained." If I say, there'd be no bishops, some might think that a step forward! But be that as it may, there wouldn't be any. Bishops are the successors of the apostles, and the chief among them, the bishop of Rome, is the successor of Peter. And if there were no bishops, there'd be no priests or deacons. And we'd be sheep without shepherds, scattered here and there. There'd be no unity and each of us would be alone, doing our own thing, constructing our own religion. Most of all, an apostle is a public, official witness to the Resurrection, and if we took them all away, we wouldn't know Christ had risen and we'd be without hope in this world. And it would be night for our souls.

No wonder, then, the Te Deum calls the apostles a "glorious choir". No wonder that every month of the year, outside March and April, the liturgy celebrates the feast of an apostle. The apostles are part and parcel of all we are and all we have as Christians, as Catholics. They're part of our prayer. Every Eucharistic Prayer recalls them. The daily Prayer of the Church takes its pattern from the way they prayed. And one day we will meet them face to face, sitting on their thrones judging the twelve tribes of Israel. It's through the apostles we access the world of grace and belong to the communion of saints. We're all of us fish swimming in the nets they have cast and when our time comes they will haul us ashore into eternity. Our fellowship is with them and theirs is with the Father and his Son, Jesus Christ (see *1 Jn* 1:3).

Be like apostles

So what is the grace of this feast of Saints Peter and Paul? It's rediscovering the apostles. It's realising, really realising, that the Church we've been called to is one, holy, catholic and apostolic. The Church is apostolic, Pope Francis has said, in three ways.[4]

She's apostolic because she's founded on the preaching and prayer of the apostles; she's a building with them as foundation.

She's apostolic, secondly, because everything the apostles left her lives on within her, because "the Church *keeps and hands on* the teaching, the 'good deposit', the salutary words she has heard from the Apostles" (*CCC* 857), "this precious treasure, which is Sacred Scripture, doctrine, the Sacraments, the ministry of Pastors, so that we can be faithful to Christ and share in his very life."[5] Yes, all these things are alive, all this apostolic legacy, and through it we can be close to Christ, have the mind and the heart of Christ. The more we accept the teaching of the Church, even if it's hard, and the more we enter her life, then the more we are with the apostles, the more with Christ, and the richer our lives will be; the more hope we will have of salvation; and the more we will have to give.

And so, thirdly, the Church is apostolic because "she is sent to bring the Gospel to all the world", because "she continues in history the mission which Jesus entrusted to the Apostles."

Let us be apostolic in all these ways. Let's not be Christians with amnesia or only taking the "feel good" bits. Let's be like the apostles who received the whole Christ and went the whole way. Let's think of them, pray to them, be pilgrims to their shrines, keep their feasts, read their writings, aspire to their closeness with Christ. Let's enter into the life and thought and prayer of the Church they founded and have never abandoned. Let's catch something of their zeal to share our faith. And may they, gathered round Mary their Queen, hold us in their prayer and pray us all together all the way to heaven.

St Benedict, Patron of Europe

First Christmas, Easter, Pentecost; then a rush of saints. That, in a very broad brush way, is the pattern of each liturgical year. Six months from Advent to Pentecost, six from Pentecost to the next Advent. First, the work of Christ for us, then the work of Christ in us. First the sowing of redemption: Jesus the seed; then the harvest of redemption: the Church and her saints. First, the lifting-up of the crucified and risen One as the Saviour, the Centre, of the world; then the drawing of the world, in the wake of saints, to that Centre and Salvation. First, everything leading to the fire of Pentecost; then everything kindled by it.

And so we see why we solemnise St Benedict now: after Easter and Pentecost, among many other saints. We see where he belongs in the pattern. Taking Pentecost as our cue, we can see him in the light of the Spirit. St Benedict had the spirit of all the just, said St Gregory; he had the spirit of Christ, that is the Holy Spirit. He was a Spirit-bearing man. Meaning what?

On Pentecost day, after the wind and tongues of fire, St Peter stood up and spoke. And he began by quoting the prophet Joel: "And in the last days it shall be, God declares, that I will pour out my Spirit upon all flesh, and your sons and your daughters shall prophesy ... I will pour out my Spirit; and they shall prophesy" (*Ac* 2: 17,18). The first gift of Pentecost is prophecy - 'prophecy' meaning here the ability to speak and act creatively for God in history, the ability to do God's work in time. St Benedict had this gift, exceptionally. His famous 'Rule' is the sign of it. That Rule was his prophetic word, his prophetic action, his creative contribution to history. Full of the energy of God's word, it fell into the soil of time, the disturbed soil of the sixth century. For a while, it seems to have disappeared, as seeds do. But then it began to grow, to flower, to bear fruit. "By this my Father is glorified, Jesus had said, that you bear much fruit, and so prove to be my disciples" (*Jn* 15:8). So it was. The Rule was a seed, the fruit was monasteries. The Rule was written in the sixth century, Benedictine monasteries have belonged to every century since - a continuing living gift.

Thanking God for today

During the seventh to ninth centuries, monasteries drawing on St Benedict's Rule begin to appear north of the Alps. The great medieval flowering followed. In the sixteenth century with the discovery of the New World, Benedictine monasteries were founded in Latin America; in the nineteenth century more especially in North America; in the latter half of the twentieth century, in Africa and Asia. Overall, just in the last ten years, despite a decline in numbers of monks and nuns, there have been some 100 new foundations of monasteries following the Rule of St Benedict - most remarkably in Kazakhstan, with plans for one in Cuba and hopes for continental China.

It is monasteries we are thanking God for today: the living presence on every continent of monasteries of men and women following the Rule of St Benedict. The Spirit of Pentecost, the spirit of prophecy, rested on St Benedict. Under that Spirit, he wrote a Rule. And from that Rule spring Benedictine monasteries. And through these monasteries, the life-giving Holy Spirit, sent at Pentecost, is ever drawing souls close to the Easter Jesus, the Son of the Father. For "God has sent the Spirit of his Son into our hearts, crying, 'Abba, Father!'" (*Ga* 4:6).

It is monasteries we are thanking the Father for today: the gift of God through St Benedict. Let's go on a little, contemplating this gift, encouraging one another to gratitude. First of all, a monastery is a gift to its own members. It is, in a phrase of the Psalms, "the place of [their] pilgrimage". It's the house of God they're privileged to live in. It's their home. It's their spiritual mother. It is the place where they experience the spiritual motherhood of the whole Church. It is where that life-giving motherhood is at work, forming them in the womb of this life to bring them forth to everlasting life. Today's readings are a guide here. A monastery is where, following Proverbs, the monk or nun can gradually learn wisdom, "understand what the fear of the Lord is, and discover the knowledge of God ... understand what virtue is, justice and fair dealing, all paths that lead to happiness" (*Pr* 2:5, 9). It is where he or she can become personally, inwardly aligned to the wisdom, the purposes, of God. It's where, following St Paul, he or she can know what it is to be "called together as parts of one body": to "bear with one another; forgive each other", to "put on love", to let Christ's peace reign, to encourage each other, to pray together, to be grateful (see *Col* 3:12-17). It's the place where, following the Gospel, we learn to serve. "For who is the greater: the one at table or the one who serves? The one at table, surely? Yet here am I among you as one who serves" (*Lk* 22:27).

The Spirit at prayer

If a monastery is first a gift to its monks, it's also one to the Church and the world. Rare is the Benedictine community that isn't surrounded - and actually kept afloat, supported, sustained, saved from any illusion of self-sufficiency - by friends and benefactors, oblates and guests. And that is a sign. "In this place I will give peace" (*Hg* 2:9). It's a sign that however weak and limited communities are they are a gift to the Church, and a gift to the world of the Church. Certainly, every Christian resource, the Church's whole potential, is needed today. But monasteries too, and monasteries not least. They are a gift of God beyond themselves. They're a presence of Christ. They're the Church in her motherliness. They're the Spirit at prayer.

So today, in this time after Pentecost, this season of saints, let us thank God for this gift. Let us ask for the grace of cherishing monasteries, holding them dear. Let us do what we can to build them up. Perhaps in that way something of the spirit of prophecy will rest on us as well.

In the 530s the Emperor Justinian built in Constantinople the great church of Holy Wisdom, Hagia Sophia, finished in five years, ten months, four days. It is one of the marvels of Christian architecture. It created a space, ruled by Christ, where, in worship, God and man could meet. But nine centuries later it became a mosque and now it's a museum. The very same years, St Benedict was writing his Rule. It too is a kind of architecture. It too creates a Christ-filled space, dedicated to wisdom, where, in worship, God and man can meet. But this space is no museum. It's alive. It's here, it's in a thousand places through the world. It is, even more, in thousands upon thousands of hearts, shaped by St Benedict's Rule. God and man are meeting.

"Let us bless the Lord. Thanks be to God."

The Transfiguration

6th August

And they went into the cloud ... and a voice came from the cloud saying, "This is my Son." (Lk 9:35-36)

Today is a great feast, the Transfiguration of the Lord. Today, a great gift is given - in the persons of Peter and John and James - to the Church: the gift of the knowledge of the Trinity: not book-knowledge, but knowledge like the knowledge a man has of his wife and a woman of her husband, a knowledge of faith and love, a knowledge had in prayer, knowledge of the Father, the Son and Holy Spirit.

Today the Church - the visible Church founded on the apostles - receives the grace of prayer; she is taught to contemplate.

"In the shining cloud the Spirit is seen; from it the voice of the Father is heard: This is my Son, my beloved, in whom is all my delight. Listen to him."

Mary had received the grace of this knowledge at the annunciation; John the Baptist received it by the river Jordan, baptising Jesus. And now Peter and John and James, too, go into the cloud and hear the Father's voice and receive - indelibly - this same knowledge.

They receive it so indelibly that even their own failure at the time of the Passion - Peter's failure especially - cannot stop them from turning back to the one they failed and running to the tomb on Easter morning. "Lord, you know that I love you." That knowledge is in these men as the character of baptism is in us. And when the Holy Spirit, not in the form of a cloud but in tongues of fire, comes down on the whole Church at Pentecost, it is Peter, standing up with the Eleven, who proclaims the Trinity and baptises the crowds into the knowledge of Father, Son and Holy Spirit, with faith and prayer.

And the gift is not recalled. The signs of this are all around us. The other day, someone told me he had become a Catholic because he saw that Catholics prayed. On the eve of this feast - another sign - in Ghana, a new Benedictine monastery was officially opened, Kristo Buase, and monks have gone from our own corner of the world to assist in its development. Surely, the eve of the Transfiguration was an appropriate day to open a house of prayer, a house dedicated to nothing but knowing the Father, the Son and the Holy Spirit. We pray Christ will fill it.

And then if we want a sign, here and now, of the power of the Transfiguration, a sign of how deeply knowledge of the Trinity is in the Church and brought to us, isn't it in the Mass? The Mass is the mountain, and the Holy Spirit comes on the gifts and changes them into the Body and

Blood of the Son, the Chosen and Beloved One. It is as if we go into the cloud, and the gift of the Transfiguration is renewed in us, and we can pray, as sons and daughters, to the Father.

So let us pray with the Church: "Lord, by the Transfiguration of your Son, make our gifts holy, and by his radiant glory free us from our sins … May the food we receive from heaven change us into his image. Amen."

The Assumption of Our Lady

15th August

The Almighty has done great things for me... (Lk 1:49).

It's good to have this feast. It's good that it comes as summer comes to its climax and the harvest begins. Christ is the "first-fruits of all who have fallen asleep" (*1 Co* 15:20), and now Mary follows him. It is the feast of "our Lady in harvest time". It's good because it takes us to the heart of the Gospel, which is Easter. This is Mary's Easter, "Easter in August". It's Mary's share in the resurrection of her Son, our Lord Jesus Christ, from the dead. It's good because the Church is having hard times in Scotland, made all too aware of its sins and weaknesses, and Mary "is the beginning and image of [the] Church's coming to perfection" (*Preface of the Mass*). She is the Church at her truest and purest. It's good because it's the patronal feast of this Cathedral. It's good most of all because it lifts our hearts to heaven, because "the sanctuary of God in heaven is opened" (*Rv* 11:19), and we glimpse where God is taking us. We see what we hope for. And we are strengthened and consoled.

"The Almighty has done great things for me" - words from Mary's Magnificat. They're youthful words. They're a great cry of joy. They burst from Mary when she was a young woman, probably only in her teens, when she had just conceived the Messiah by the power of the Holy Spirit, and knew she was "blessed among women" (*Lk* 1:42). And the Liturgy, inspired by the same Holy Spirit, puts them on her lips again today - when she is old. Or better, when her Son is taking her up, body and soul, into the everlasting youthfulness of heaven.

"The Almighty has done great things for me." Indeed he has. From the first moment of her existence, he freed her from the guilt of original sin and filled her with sanctifying grace. When "the age for love" (*Ez* 16:8) came, he invited her to become the mother of his only-begotten Son and she conceived by the power of the Holy Spirit. With divine courtesy, he did not allow this to take away her virginity but instead consecrated it (*non minuit sed sacravit*), and so this mother is a virgin before, during and after childbirth - a combination of opposites only God's power could work. He entrusted the upbringing of Jesus to her and Joseph. He made her intervention at Cana the occasion of Jesus's first miracle or sign. By his will, she stood at the foot of the Cross, uniting herself to Christ's sacrifice and receiving the beloved disciple as her son. When the Holy Spirit was sent at Pentecost, it was her prayers that had helped prepare the space for him.

Dying in love

"The Almighty has done great things for me." It's the theme-song of her life.

And today she sings it again. Today she is taken up, body and soul, into heaven. It has been discussed among the theologians whether Mary was taken up while still alive or if she first died. The majority view is that she did die. Pope John Paul II certainly endorsed this view. She shared in the death and resurrection of her Son. How could it be otherwise? Having been freed from original sin, dying had no aspect of a punishment for her. Rather, "involved in Christ's redemptive work and associated with his saving sacrifice, Mary was able to share in his suffering and death for the sake of humanity's redemption". Her dying shared in the redeeming character of Christ's. "Whatever from the physical point of view was the organic, biological cause of the end of her bodily life", "it is more important to look for the Blessed Virgin's spiritual attitude at the moment of her departure from this world" (John Paul II, *General Audience*, 25th June 1997). St Francis de Sales speaks of her dying "in love, from love, and through love" - so far can the love of Christ take hold of a human being. The Eastern Church speaks of Mary's 'dormition', her falling asleep. So, for all the fire of her love, this was a gentle death, a falling asleep in the Lord. And Pope John Paul added a beautiful thing here. Mary has already shared humanity's common destiny. She knows it from the inside, therefore. So, she can be our mother then in a very powerful way. Hence our words: "pray for us sinners now and at the hour of our death."

Sharing in Christ's death, then, she was ready to share in his Resurrection. "The Almighty has done great things for me." The Assumption, we can say, is the greatest and the last of all those "great things". By the power of God, the separation of her body and soul is overcome. She is spared "the corruption of the tomb" (*Preface*). She is filled with the glory of God, body and soul. She is taken into the Father's arms, completely conformed to Christ, her whole being transfused by the Holy Spirit. Words fail here. And since no one is closer to us than God, and Mary very close to him, she can come very close to us, "the highest after Christ and the closest to us" (Paul VI). "The clarity in her God-seeing mind enables her to perceive our needs, the charity in her God-fired heart moves her to meet them" (John Saward). She is "the sign of sure hope and comfort to God's pilgrim people" (*Preface*), a mother for all our needs.

The first disciple of Christ

"The Almighty has done great things for me." Mary is the type or symbol, the concentration in one person, of the Church. So what the Almighty has done for her, he does for the Church. Mary is the first and most thorough disciple of Christ, the first of a long line in which we want to stand too. What the Almighty does for her in 'bold', as it were, what he does for her in 'high definition', he does for the Church and for each of us. This is what we're offered by this feast: a refreshing sense of the power and wisdom and mercy and love of the Father. That he has done and does and will do great things for *us*. That we too, at our level, in our place, can be a theatre, a focus, a locus, of this same divine action. This is why at Evening Prayer every day, the Divine Office gives *us* the Magnificat too, to echo Mary. The Father sanctifies us in baptism, as he sanctified her at her conception. The Father makes the Church and each of us bearers of Christ to the world, as he made her. The Father has the Church "keep intact faith, firm hope and sincere charity" (Vatican II, *Lumen Gentium* 64), after the image of Mary "ever-virgin". The Father gives us strength to accept the Cross into our lives, so that our hearts may be enlarged with divine compassion, as hers. The Father gives us the power to call the Holy Spirit down into the world from the heart of the Church, as she did. And the Almighty will lead us through the valley of the shadow of death to the world of life everlasting and resurrection, as, to the joy of the angels, he leads her today.

"The Almighty has done great things for me." So many "things" can conspire to take this song out of our hearts and off our lips. May today, may Mary, bring it to life in us again!

Exaltation of the Holy Cross

Today is the feast of the Exaltation or Triumph of the Holy Cross. It's a feast with complex origins and multiple associations. It has connections with what was thought to be the discovery of the Cross on which Christ died by the Empress Helena in *c.*327, with the dedication of the basilica erected at the supposed location of Calvary in Jerusalem, the Martyrium, in 335, with the act of the lifting-up of the relic of the Cross in that church for the veneration of the faithful, which would take place on 14th September, and with the recovery of that relic from the Persians by the Emperor Heraclius in 630. These things, however, merely occasioned the feast and its spread; they are not its object. From the historical point of view, this feast incorporates into the liturgy the ancient devotion to the Cross and later Crucifix which is so central to the symbolic world of Christianity. It is an early parallel to the way in which the liturgy has incorporated in the feast of the Holy Trinity the early medieval devotion to the Mystery of the Three in One, or in the feast of Corpus Christi the high medieval delight in appreciation of the sacramental presence of Christ and the Eucharist, or in the feast of the Sacred Heart the seventeenth century appreciation of the unfathomable depth of love pierced by the soldier's spear. But, at the deeper level of the mystery being celebrated, it is simplest perhaps to think of today's feast as Good Friday in autumn. Here we are just prior to the autumn equinox celebrating the same mystery of redemption that was celebrated just after the spring equinox. The approach, the 'theme', the 'spirituality' is the same. At the ritual level, the primary 'lifting-up' of the Cross, its 'showing' in view of adoration, actually takes place in the liturgy of Good Friday. What we are remembering today, then, is the redemption won for us by Christ on and through the Cross, by way of the Cross. And the grace we are asking is its completion in heaven.

Brushing off the dust

If we are practical people and want something to do, then it is a good day for what Roland Walls called brushing the dust off our signs of the Cross, for banishing the senseless squiggle from our lives.

Another reflection occurs to me. I'm always fascinated by how, looking at reality of any kind, even, I think, material reality, one finds this structure of "the whole in the part". I suppose a human cell, with its DNA, is a good example at the level of biology. But the pattern seems at its strongest when we look at the mysteries of the faith, especially as expressed in the liturgy. What we are celebrating always is God's great work of our redemption, our being set free and given a life that outlives death and is even a share in the life of God. *O God, from whom both redemption comes to us and adoption is fulfilled for us.* And in each 'part' of, for example, the liturgical year, in each 'particular', the whole is present. Each 'part' turns out to be a symbol, something which throws together, gathers the scattered into one. And so, in a real sense, the whole of redemption is in the Cross, and therefore on Good Friday and today's feast. In another sense, it is wholly in the empty tomb or rather in the Resurrection, and therefore 'available' on Easter Sunday and in Eastertide. In another way, it is completely present in the Eucharist. In another way again in the Incarnation as manifested at Christmas and Epiphany. In another way, in the gift of the Spirit - the forgiveness of sins in person - renewed at Pentecost. In another way, in the pierced Heart and so on.

One or other of these symbols may have particular eloquence for us as individuals, or for Christians *en masse* at a particular period of history. Sometimes, saints are shaped and 'made' by one or other of these parts, but it is always by a part, because in that part is the whole. This is not a phenomenon unique to Western Christianity either. Think of how the Transfiguration 'transfixed' Athonite monks of the fourteenth/fifteenth centuries. The healthy thing about a spiritual life centred on the liturgy and rhythmed by the liturgical year is that it's fed by all the symbols, by the whole in each of its parts. It is guaranteed a balanced diet. Today, then, we are reminded that the whole is in and from the Cross. *O Crux ave, spes unica.*

The victory of Good Friday

There is a traditional association between St Benedict and the Cross. Today's feast, we say, begins the monastic Lent, a little turn towards next year's Easter. Strictly speaking, this is coincidental. The ides of September (the 13th) are a cardinal point in St Benedict's year, but he would not have known this feast on this date. The wider association comes, I suppose, from the Dialogues, where the sign of the Cross is seen to be one of St Benedict's weapons against the Evil One. And then there's St Benedict's medal. The monk, we know, is a cross-bearer (a *staurophore*). "If any man would come after me ..." Life through death is the whole idea of the monastic way. We share by patience in the sufferings of Christ ... The monk is meant to be marked with the sign of the Cross and to be sensitive to the glory hidden in the Cross.

On the Cross, we see Christ's love. And the Rule is a guide to loving, to cruciform loving, that is, loving which has, in its small way, the same form as the love Christ showed on the Cross. All the spiritual emphases that emerge from the Rule could be unified around this. What does St Benedict advocate if not humble love, feet-washing love, reverent love of God (the vertical) and hard-working love (the horizontal). The Rule, in its way, is there to bring the mystery of the Cross from faith and liturgy to everyday living. One would even see that the Cross the monk carries and that seals him for redemption *is* the Rule, that is the love the Rule teaches.

But this is the feast of the *triumph* of the Cross, its lifting-up, exalting, glorification; the Cross as a boast à la St Paul. Yes, life is a battle and we're meant to win. We must never forget that. Victory is what we're after: the victory, precisely, of the Cross, that is to say, of Christ's humble love. This is what we find it so hard to accept. Even as Christians, we so easily misconstrue the victory. The Church, as a whole, and each community within it, and each member of it, is signed with the sign of the Cross. And NO OTHER victory is promised us, this side of the End, than the victory of cruciform love. The victory of Good Friday: "Father, into your hands, I commend my spirit." "Father, forgive them, for they know not what they do." The vertical and the horizontal. Prayer and forgiveness. No other victory than the victory of Good Friday; and the victory of Good Friday a light that can never be put out, the tree of life that can never be hewn down.

What the Cross teaches us is to look beyond appearances. I suppose we all of us have visions of victory, and not just for ourselves, but for the Church and for Christ. It may be Parliament outlawing abortion or fearless bishops thundering against immorality or Muslims by the million begging for baptism or overflowing seminaries or Carmels being established in every village in Scotland, so many are thirsting for the contemplative life. Of course, such things can happen and if they do, can have the grace of God within them, be signs of the Resurrection at work in history. I think many a seed must have been sown in the Jubilee year, to sprout in the decades hence: even in the Western world or in the Muslim world. The seventeenth century saw a more thorough Christianisation of European society than the fifteenth. The nineteenth century was one of the great centuries of Christian history and there was far more Christianity slopping around in the 1870s than in the 1770s. Couldn't the twenty-first century see yet another revival? We shall see.

May we live under the sign of the Cross

But, in the end, all those things are in God's hands, and the victory of the Cross is something always and everywhere present, not dependent on the vicissitudes of history. It is always hidden, and always there. And who can say, in a sense, where it is? "The Kingdom of God does not admit of observation." A convent of nuns, which has run its course and done its work, and 'dies', may in its dying be closer to Christ than it ever was in its living. The contemplative life, in particular, has to be something hidden and fragile and suffering. And if in the West, now, that often takes the form of ageing and diminishing, maybe that is the very truest expression of cruciform love, of standing with the Marys and John. One of the great nineteenth-century political commentators, de Tocqueville it may have been, famously said of Russia: when it is strong it is never as strong as it looks and when it is weak it is never as weak as it looks. This seems, to me, even truer of the Church. If there is the humble love of the crucified Christ in the strong new and bursting movements, it's *that* which is to be hailed. And if there is patience and prayer in a weak and dying community, there is no need for tears if it dies, because it is dying in God and life will come from it. "When I am weak, then I am strong."

May the Cross of Christ deliver us from all false expectations and all rash judgements, Imagine an old monk who only seems interested in food and sleep and a young one who only seems interested in prayer. Who is closer to the triumph of the Cross? "We have this treasure in clay jars, so that it may be made clear that this extraordinary power belongs to God and does not come from us." St Paul, if anyone, grasped and lived the paradox of the Cross.

So, "loving humility is a terrible force; there's nothing on earth that can resist it." So said Dostoevsky. It is the one true victory, God's, and there's no point bothering about any other or, to be honest, about all the evil in the world. It has been defeated. May we live under the sign of the Cross!

St Michael
and all Angels

The Roman Calendar devotes this day to the three archangels known from Scripture: Michael, Gabriel and Raphael. The Benedictine Calendar is more global. It entitles the feast St Michael and All Angels. It invites us, therefore - and its Collect too - to consider the angelic world as a whole, and its interaction with the world we think of as our own.

That angels are is an article of faith. Bodiless persons, pure spirits, invisible beings; powerful, numerous, "ministering spirits sent forth to serve" (*Hb* 1:14); presences in the physical world, influences on human history, key figures in the story of salvation; our helpers, our enlighteners, guides towards the joy of heaven: such are the things Scripture and Tradition tell us. Yes, but peripheral, some would say, and dispensable: part of the background clutter our faith would travel lighter and further without. But are background and periphery really dispensable? What would an artist say? The Lord, the Father, the Spirit, the Church, the Eucharist, the Sacraments, life in Christ: these are the centre and hold the foreground, certainly. But believe in the angels, and you will not find yourself distracted from these things, but rather find those things more centred in yourself. "The angels keep their ancient places" is a familiar line from Francis Thompson, and a true one. But they keep other things as well. They, and only they, I think, keep some vital things alive in our hearts, for lack of which we will be less alive. A person who believes in angels - I mean really, sensitively, intelligently - can be more of a person than one who doesn't. It makes a difference.

Three things in particular one might mention that the angels keep alive in us: our need for help, possibilities of insight, and the reality of joy.

We are rescued - more than we know

First, our need for help, or better, the presence of help. In his Rule (1:4), St Benedict uses the lovely phrase *multorum solacium*: the help, support, solace of many (that is, brethren). It's the comfort of the cenobite. "Brother helping brother is a strong defence", says Proverbs. What monk or lay person hasn't experienced this? But we have angelic brothers, too, brethren in the Mystical Body. We entangle ourselves, we imperil ourselves, and, when all is said and done, our world is a threatening place. We can't possibly go it alone. But "the Lord rescues the souls of his servants and those who hide in him will not be condemned", says the Psalm (*Ps* 33:23). And he rescues them through their brothers, through the angels: "God defends his chosen ones in the Church, in troubled times he is himself their shield, and through the watchful care of angels he protects them. He presents the angels to his own as servants ... to further their salvation, to report their needs" (Richard of St Victor).

The Bible says it again and again. An angel rescued Lot. An angel stopped Abraham sacrificing Isaac. An angel led Israel through the desert. An angel helped Elijah on the way to Horeb. An angel protected Shadrach, Mishach and Abednego. An angel took Habbakuk by the hair and brought Daniel dinner. An angel strengthened Judas Maccabeus. An angel counselled Joseph when the Child's life was under threat. Angels ministered to the Lord in the desert. An angel took Peter out of prison. In every case, help was needed, consciously or not. And help was given. But mediated help, angelic help. Creation was sent to rescue creation, servants sent to fellow-servants. Belief in the angels will keep our awareness of these things alive, will keep us in the truth. "Over all the doings of men," wrote Max Picard, "there is mercy beforehand, a great pre-forgiving. How many dreadful things pass through man's soul, through his mind, between 6 o'clock in the morning when he awakens and 10 o'clock in the evening when he falls asleep! But man is not able to do all these dreadful things, he is protected against himself. We are rescued - more than we know." Yes, "the Lord rescues the souls of his servants", and the angels are the symbols and agents of this. We have "the solace of many".

Seeing the inside

Then, possibilities of insight: of the sight of what's within, of the inscape of things. Let me tell a story our Novice Master once told me. It concerned Jean Vanier, the founder of L'Arche. He was sending someone to an airport to collect a visitor. "What does he look like?" asked the emissary. "Oh," said Vanier, "he's a beautiful young man: he has a beautiful soul, and his soul is in his eyes." Some use as a description! But, they did meet up. And the strange thing was that the young man was well over 6 foot tall and had a ponytail. Asked for a description, that's what we would have mentioned. Jean Vanier, though, had seen something quite different. He had simply seen the manifestation of soul. He'd seen the inside, as it were. And isn't this precisely what the monastic tradition, since Evagrius, calls "the contemplation of created realities"? And who, in that same tradition, are the symbols, guardians, instruments of such a contemplation, such an insight? The angels.

"If you pray in all truth," wrote Evagrius (*Chapters on Prayer* 80), "you will come upon a deep sense of confidence. Then the angels will walk with you and enlighten you concerning the meaning of created things." That is, they will show you the 'inscape' of things, persons, events and situations. "What will it be to look / From God's side even of such a simple thing?" asked Alice Meynell in a poem on a daisy. And isn't that where the angels lead us? To see the soul in the eyes or an empty tomb as the place of resurrection? St Thomas and his followers say the same. Angelic guardianship "aims at enlightenment ... as to its final, chief effect" (*Summa Theologiae* I, 113, 5, ad 2). Indeed, wrote Anscar Vonier, "according to St Thomas, it is not too much to say that the human race is kept in mental equilibrium through the unceasing watchfulness of the good spirits." Beyond their natural knowledge, they enjoy another, one that is the source of their supernatural happiness, the knowledge "by which they see the Word and things in the Word" (ibid. 1, 57, 5). And this they can share with us, as they shared it with Mary, with the shepherds, with the women at the tomb, with the disciples gazing after the ascending Christ. They lead us to the contemplation of the Mystery as it unfolds in the heart of the world and of men. Their presence is our possibility of insight.

The reality of joy

Lastly, the reality of joy. Angels abound, says the Tradition. "Turn but a stone and start a wing." They fill churches and holy places. "May your holy angels dwell here and keep us in peace", we pray in the evening. Can't we imagine our house filling up with them at that moment? Or there is the invariable mention of them at the climax of the Preface of the Eucharistic Prayer. Mightn't that be their cue? Suddenly the sanctuary is thick with them: concelebrating angels, as the Church is bold enough to call them. And what of the physical world? What of the woods, for example? Who doesn't think of woods as somehow full? Full of what? Full of fairies and leprechauns? Or, more soberly, full of the spirits of their ancient human inhabitants? Or can't we say, full of angels? Newman goes further (*The Powers of Nature*, PPS II, XXIX): "Every breath of air and ray of light and heat, every beautiful prospect, is, as it were, the skirts of their garments, the waving of the robes of those whose faces see God in heaven." And that, if we think it through, means joy. Angels see God. Angels are in joy. And the world is full of angels. Therefore, full of joy. "Reality is joy," said Paul Couturier. But by the ministry of angels. We cannot, usually, 'see' this physically, nor appropriate it emotionally or psychologically. We cannot, at those levels of our being, as yet 'enter into' joy. But the angels are a pledge that the joy is there, and waiting to be entered. If we allow the angels to "keep their ancient places", keep them in our hearts, then we are keeping joy in our hearts. And we will have experience not only of help, not only of illumination, but of having "the roads to Sion" in our hearts, walking "with ever growing strength" till "we see the God of gods in Sion" (*Ps* 83:6, 8) and enter into joy among the angels.

May this feast, then, revive our faith, and the indwelling Spirit assure us "companionship with angels" (St Basil, *On the Holy Spirit*, 23).

Guardian Angels

2nd October

On 29th September the Church keeps the feast of the Archangels Michael, Gabriel and Raphael; on 2nd October, she remembers the Guardian Angels. This, then, is an appropriate moment for thinking about the angels.

No doubt there are many ways of doing this, and each of us can follow his own preference. My own way is to turn to this one angel to whom I have been entrusted and think simply about him.

It has for long been the conviction of the Church that each of us has such a guardian angel. The Jews of our Lord's time believed this, and our Lord confirmed that belief when he said: "See that you never despise any of these little ones" - that is children, but also metaphorically, believers - "for I tell you that their angels in heaven are continually in the presence of my Father in heaven." "No one mindful of these words of the Lord," says St Basil, "can deny that an angel is present to each person, as a kind of pedagogue and shepherd, guiding his living." And if an angel is present to each person, an angel is present to me. And I can turn my mind to him.

A remarkable being

And my first thought, simply, is, what a remarkable being he must be. He is a pure spirit, which is why I cannot see him with my two eyes. He does not have a body. He is not a part of the material world. And if he is a spirit, he's a person. He's not an impersonal force. He's an individual being of a rational nature. He has a mind and a will of his own. He is not an automaton. He's an independent centre, free. He thinks; he makes decisions; he acts. He has a character of his own. He is also greatly more powerful than I am, in terms of spiritual power. He knows more. The range of his mind is far greater than mine; its operation far faster. He can penetrate into any matter so thoroughly and rapidly, that he never has to reverse a decision. He's also superior to me in point of time. It is true he has a beginning; he is not eternal, but it also seems that he has existed at least as long as our universe. He existed when the "Big Bang" happened, if it did. He existed when the first signs of life appeared, when the first men appeared. He has existed through all the centuries of human history. The only qualification to be made here is that an angel's experience of time is quite different from a man's. It is not measured by days and nights, weeks, years, centuries even. An angel lives in angelic time, which Cardinal Newman describes as "measured by the living thought alone" - a difficult idea to grasp and one which need not detain us.

A servant of God

My second thought is that this remarkable being, this spirit-friend of mine, is above all a servant of God. He is among the "thousand thousands ... the ten thousand times ten thousand" whom Daniel saw standing before the Ancient of Days and 'serving' Him. He is there, of course, by the mercy of God, but he is also there by choice. He has been 'tested' and found 'worthy'. The story of the human race opens with a test and so does the story of the angelic race. We do not know precisely what form this testing of the angels took. St Thomas Aquinas says that the testing of the angels was the revelation of the supernatural. By "the supernatural", he means God's free and gracious plan "to unite everything in Christ, things in heaven and things on earth", to raise both angels and men above their natural capacities and make them "partakers of the divine nature". The angels were offered this, called to it. Their vocation was shown to them. They were called not to rest in whatever excellence belongs to them by nature. They were called out of their own sphere into a higher one, which was at the same time more universal, involving community with lower spirits, with man. They were called at one and the same time to a greater glory and a new humility. They were faced with the sovereign freedom of Almighty God, the "ever-greater".

Perhaps they were shown human nature joined to the Second Person of the Trinity and lifted far above them; perhaps they were shown Mary, a merely human being but one day destined to be their Queen and nearer God than they were. We don't know. We only know that, somehow, they were called; love and obedience were asked of them. And at that moment, the great split in the angelic world took place. Lucifer and his angels cried out "I shall not serve" and went into rebellion, into active opposition to God's plan of redemption, into hell. Michael and his angels cried out "Who is like God?" and chose to serve. Among them was my angel. My angel chose God. He chose to serve.

The choice was for ever. It opened heaven to him, the vision of God and torrential joy. He became "a ministering" - literally, liturgical - spirit, waiting to be "sent forth to serve, for the sake of those who are to obtain salvation".

Angel of God, my friend

And so he became, in the fullness of time, an agent of God's redemptive providence towards the human race. He co-operated willingly in the evolution of planet earth, knowing it was destined to be the home of creatures dear to God. He went about unknown missions in the long centuries between the first sin of those creatures and the call of Abraham. He watched over the Chosen

People. He was with them when they came out of Egypt; he was one of the angels mediating the law to Moses; he strengthened the hands of those who fought their way into the Promised Land. He rejoiced at the immaculate conception of a Jewish girl called Mary, knowing that this was the dawn of salvation, and when that girl, in time, conceived by the Holy Spirit and the Son of God entered the human race, my angel heard God say "Worship Him!" - and he did. Perhaps he was among the "multitude of the heavenly host" on the first Christmas night singing "Glory to God in the highest and peace among men on earth". Perhaps he was among the angels who ministered to Christ in the desert after his fast of forty days. Certainly, now, after the Ascension, he stands among the "many angels, numbering myriads of myriads and thousands of thousands, saying with a loud voice 'Worthy is the Lamb who was slain, to receive power … and honour and glory and blessing!'" Certainly, again, he will be among the angels who, at the end of this world's time, will come with Christ in the glory of the Father, and "gather his elect from the four winds, from the ends of the earth to the ends of heaven!" (*Mk* 13:27)

And so I come back to where I began. This remarkable being, this faithful servant of God, is also my friend. Extraordinary though it may sound, it is his joy to serve me, to be a "fellow servant" with me. It is his joy to be to me an angel of peace, and of penitence, and of prayer, protecting me from trouble, urging me back to God when I sin, taking my prayers to God and God's answer to me. He does all this. He does all unobtrusively, uninterruptedly. There is a constant flow from him to me, a constant friendship. He is always beside me. He is with me now, and I hope is pleased that for once I have not forgotten him.

All Saints

In this solemnity we are celebrating those holy men and women of every time and place who have lived the beatitudes and been given the kingdom. We are celebrating all those, known and unknown, who now see God, who see him as he is, who stand before the Throne and the Lamb (the Father and the Son) and cry out in the Spirit with a loud cry: "Victory to our God who sits upon the throne and to the Lamb." We are celebrating their care for us, their cry to us to lift up our hearts, that heavenly pull on the believing heart that the thought of God's glory should be.

Three thoughts come to mind. First, what confidence in God this feast should rouse in us. It's a victory we are celebrating, the victory of the grace and mercy of God. A saint is not a Superman. A saint is not necessarily or normally someone who captures the public eye and leaves such a mark on his time that even journalists or secular historians must bow before him. A saint is a human being who has come to belong wholly to God. That is holiness. A saint is someone in whose life love has the last word. A saint is someone who, after many misgivings perhaps, many misunderstandings and mistakes, after detours and difficulties, after repeated conversions and fresh starts, has at last found his way to the Father's house and to what it means to be a human being, made in the image and likeness of God. He or she is a witness, simply, that God's forgiving love, God's fatherly Providence and God's creating and predestining will is *the* factor in every life. "Even to old age I am He, and to grey hairs I will carry you. I have made, and I will bear; I will carry and will save" (*Is* 46:4).

Secret passwords

And out of this comes a second thought: if this is how it is, how can we not desire to give our lives over to the purposes of God? "Surely everyone who entertains this hope must purify himself, must try to be as pure as Christ" (*1 Jn* 3:3). At the very least obedience of ourselves to God can claim to be enlightened self-interest. But there's nothing to stop it being love. Why should we cling on to anything except the lasting? Why not accept the Beatitudes into our lives? They are the secret passwords into God's kingdom, into the victory, into the mercy. Let's want to be holy!

Then, a last thought. The saints in heaven are not disconnected one from another, not just a crowd of isolated individuals. As the liturgy is at pains to point out, we are celebrating a city. They are fellow citizens one of another. They form a city, they form a whole. They are a world. They are a church, the Church triumphant. They are humanity come to its goal. They are the Holy City, the new Jerusalem, lit by the glory of God, not only in their relations with him but in their relations one to another and for ever. And there is a message for us in this. Think of a city. Think of London, for instance. There's much that impresses, much to admire. Here we are at the centre of political and economic and social life. Here are people beyond counting. But there's one thing one can't help noticing. Not just the freneticism, not just the ubiquitous appeal to the sordid and the superficial, not just the pervasive threat of crime and terrorism, not even the people rolled up in blankets trying to sleep on the steps of theatres or shops, but something more diffuse and deeper. Here are individuals, couples, small groups all busy with their own tasks, and - which is the point - sealed off one from another. Here is a "great crowd" but not united. Here are people but not a community. Or here is a community but not communion. It's not that there is no civility. It's not that there isn't an urge to kindness in many hearts. But something - fear mainly - stops it breaking into flower. Travel on an underground train late at night. No one looks at each other. Eyes are switched off. They don't acknowledge the other. The other, after all, might have a knife, and be after your wallet or your body. The cities of men are paradoxical places. They express a desire they can't fulfil, and even oppose. And the result is not a city but disconnection.

In the City of God, we believe, it's otherwise. The eyes of the saints see God; they see God in each other and each other in God. Their eyes are light and their hearts are open, and each knows the other and is happy to know all and to be known. Each is himself and each is in communion - the fellowship of the Holy Spirit.

And so let's take a resolve from this feast. Confidence in God, and a thirst for holiness; and a third thing too. Each of us lives in a community, or in more than one. And each of these communities has a potential to become an outpost of the Jerusalem above, an embassy of heaven. Each of these has room for a little more mutual respect and mutual love, or rather we ... "I have chosen to live on the threshold of God's house," says the Psalmist. And so when Christ comes, with all his saints, he will not be coming to strangers.

All Souls

I have made your name known to them and will continue to make it known so that the love with which you loved me may be in them, and so that I may be in them (Jn 17:26).

These are the last words of Jesus' last prayer for the Church, for us. They are his last will for the Church. Except that, given who He is, one shouldn't say "last". They express his continuing will and prayer for us. He has risen from the dead and lives for ever to intercede for us, and the words he spoke express his enduring will.

"... so that the love with which you loved me may be in them, and so that I may be in them." Jesus's will, Jesus's prayer is that the Father's love for the Son, and he himself, may be in us - that is, in those who have believed as a result of the apostles' witness to him. His will, his prayer is that the community of believers, the Church, may be filled, sustained, carried, surrounded by the love of the Father and by his own presence - by, we can say, the Trinity itself: the Father's love for the Son being the Holy Spirit, Love in person.

We are, in St Cyprian's famous words, "a people made one by the unity of the Father, the Son and the Holy Spirit". And for "unity", one could read "charity", *caritas*, the love of God. This is some vision. Dying, death and the dead are not subjects we enjoy engaging with. We shrink from them. We shrink from them because death seems stronger than us.

But today, All Souls, the Commemoration of the Faithful Departed, the love with which the Father loves the Son, the love with which the Son gave his life on the cross, the love which raised him from the dead, the love which is the Holy Spirit, meets the kingdom of the dead.

"For love is strong as death," says the Song of Songs in a famous line, "passion fierce as the grave." But all the love I may have for a mother or a spouse or children or a friend cannot prevent them dying, cannot call them back from the world of the dead. There is only one love that can do this: the love with which the Father loves the Son, the love with which the Son died, the love which raised him from the dead.

And this love, Jesus prays, Jesus prays with no possibility of his prayer being unheard, is the love in us, in those who believe, in his mystical Body, the Church. It is, in St Paul's terms, the love of God poured into our hearts by the Holy Spirit.

Death will be nothing to fear, simply a gateway to life

In some ways, our world handles dying better than ever. In other ways, it appears quite helpless. Not so the Church of Christ, the Body of the Risen One. There are things no amount of human efficiency can do; there are things only faith, hope and love - the life of the Spirit - can do. The prayers and sacraments, the funeral and burial rites, the Masses, the suffrages, the alms, the indulgences even with which Mother Church surrounds the dying and the dead are the outward manifestations of the love with which the Father loved the Son and raised him from the dead as a life-giving Spirit. They are the power of resurrection. Every day - but today, All Souls, and throughout November in a special way - we live in time; and seasons help us - this love invades the kingdom of the dead: the departed dear to us, the departed known only to God.

This love, stronger than death, lives in the saints whom we remembered yesterday. It lives in all those at peace with God while still being purified, the Holy Souls. And it lives in us. The saints' love prays for us, still on pilgrimage, and for those in the place of purification. The love in the Holy Souls prays for us too, and our love prays for them. It is the prayer of Jesus fulfilled: "that the love with which you loved me may be in them, and that I may be in them."

We, Catholic Christians at the beginning of the third millennium, have been called most eloquently by John Paul II and his successors to be witnesses of this love. It is within us, within us as a body, within us, please God, as individuals. It is a power. It is a talent. It has myriad expressions. We will be judged on our use or neglect of it. And one way we may use it, one way we may with a very specific effect witness to it, is in not shrinking from dying and death and the dead, but by this love, this prayer. And if we have died already, died the death of this love, death will be nothing to fear, simply a gateway to life.

Christic the King

The solemnity of Christ the King[6] has sometimes been called an "idea-feast". It is nothing of the kind. It is the feast of a reality. The reality of Christ's kingship, Christ's kingdom. A bewildering, mysterious reality, even a joke sometimes (at the foot of the Cross, for example), and yet more real than any other kingship or kingdom there has ever been. A hidden king, but visible in his sacraments. A king who has come, but is coming again. A kingdom like and unlike, friend and foe to, every other kingdom. A kingdom here and not here, in the world but not of it. The paradoxes are endless.

And this is what we feast, affirming. Yes, first of all affirming, acclaiming this king and his kingdom, simply and joyfully. He / it was foreshadowed in the kingship of David, and promised by the prophets, and now he / it has come. "I myself will pasture my sheep, I myself will show them where to rest - it is the Lord who speaks. I shall look for the lost one, bring back the stray, bandage the wounded and make the weak strong." G. K. Chesterton once remarked that only belonging to the Church sets one free from the degrading slavery of being a child of one's times. And so it is. Affirming, acclaiming this King - "You are the Christ, the true King" - loosens the clutches of all the other competing kingdoms: public opinion, totalitarian governments, market forces, the dogmas of the age, our own addictions, King sin and King death. They all have their day and their sway, but there is something else abroad as well, subverting them all. There is a freedom and a clarity and a kingship of soul in the gift of Jesus the King. And "You are the Christ, the true King" is the song of those set free by belief. It's a song most of all for times of distress, when the powers of the world seem to rule everything and leave us no space. "Swear by the genius of Caesar, curse Christ," said the pro-consul to the aged bishop of Smyrna. "For eighty-six years," came Polycarp's magnificent reply, "I have been his servant, and he has done me no wrong, and how can I blaspheme my King who has saved me?" "I myself will pasture my sheep, I myself will show them where to rest." First of all today, we are affirming: "Christ is King."

A Kingdom in waiting

Secondly we're praying. "Thy kingdom come", we say. The kingdom is only present in mystery as yet. It is a kingdom in waiting. "After that, says St Paul, will come the end, when he hands over the kingdom to God the Father, having done away with every sovereignty, authority and power", when even death, the last enemy, will be destroyed. And so we pray. When we pray for each other, when we pray for the dead, when we pray for peace and justice, we are praying, "Thy kingdom come." When we pray, "Have mercy on me, a sinner", we are praying, "Thy kingdom come." We can pray as St Bernard prayed: "And now, Lord Jesus, come and remove the stumbling blocks within the kingdom which is my soul, so that you who ought to may reign in it. Greed comes along and claims its throne in me; arrogance wants to dominate me; pride would be my king. Comfort and pleasure say: We shall reign! Ambition, detraction, envy, anger fight within me for supremacy, and seem to have me entirely in their power. But I resist in so far as I can; I struggle against them insofar as I receive your help. I protest that Jesus is my Lord. I keep myself for him; I acknowledge his rights over me. To me he is God; to me he is Lord; and I declare, I will have no king but the Lord Jesus! Come then, Lord, rout them by your power and you will reign in me, for you are my King and my God, who grant victories to Jacob."

So thirdly, surely, we'll find ourselves resolving. We'll find ourselves wanting to live free, with kingship over ourselves, free enough therefore to give ourselves in humble love. "Come, you whom my Father has blessed, take for your heritage the kingdom prepared for you since the foundation of the world. For I was hungry and you gave me food; I was thirsty and you gave me drink; I was a stranger and you made me welcome; naked and you clothed me, sick and you visited me, in prison and you came to see me." That is the kingdom and the kingship of Christ. Next Sunday it is Advent, and a new liturgical year. At the beginning of Matthew's Gospel stand the Beatitudes, at the end these works of mercy. At the beginning, "Blessed are the poor in spirit, for theirs is the kingdom of heaven." At the end, "And the King will answer, 'I tell you solemnly, insofar as you did this to one of the least of these brothers of mine, you did it to me.'" And in the middle comes the acclamation of St Peter, "You are the Christ, the messianic King, the Son of God." Let us live what we hear, proud to have Christ as our King.

Endnotes

1. The Most Holy Trinity (Year A): *Ex* 34:4-6, 8-9; *2 Co* 13: 11-13; *Jn* 3:16-18.

2. The Most Holy Body and Blood of Christ (Year B): *Ex* 24:3-8; *Hb* 9:11-15); *Mk* 14:12-16, 22-26.

3. The Most Sacred Heart of Jesus: *Ez* 34:11-16; *Rm* 5:5-11; *Lk* 15:3-7.

4. Francis, General Audience (16th October 2013).

5. Ibid.

6. Our Lord Jesus Christ, King of the Universe (Year A) *Ez* 34:11-12, 15-17; *1 Co* 15:20-26, 28; *Mt* 25:31-46.